ackee for the soul

Andrew Malcom
Ackee For The Soul

Published by Spines
ISBN: 979-8-89383-078-1

ackee for the soul

Life Lessons from Xaymaca - Jamaica

andrew malcolm

contents

A wonderful collection of the wisdom passed on to me by my elders.
I love you, and for those of you who have transitioned, rest well.

foreword

The ackee fruit holds its origins in West Africa and was most likely brought to Jamaica in the mid-18th century.

Across the African continent, it is known by many names – "isin", "atsa", "finsan", and "kyira". Its scientific name "Blighia Sapida" pays homage to Captain William Bligh, a British naval officer who took the fruit from Jamaica to the Royal Botanic Gardens in Kew, England, in 1793.

I had an interesting conversation with a Ghanaian gentleman several years ago. I was informed that the fruit is also used in West Africa for traditional medicine, primarily for colds and fevers. Up until that point, I just thought of it as a tasty fruit that went well with codfish and dumplings for a delicious dinner.

Sometimes, I'd enjoy this delicious meal at my grandmother's home. I have very fond memories. I was chasing chickens, going down to the river and playing with my cousins. With my naturally curious mind, I questioned her constantly, and she would sometimes answer with sayings called proverbs. As a child, I just thought it was just adults being funny. Now, as an adult, I see how wise they were and still are.

This is my compilation of proverbs. Most of which I heard from the elders, including my grandmother, and some I picked up along the way. Whether as nourishment, medicine (or just plain laughter), you absolutely must do one thing.

ENJOY

1
"cack mout kill cack"

Translation: The rooster was killed by his own mouth. (The butcher would not have known where to find him if he had not opened his mouth to crow.)

Explanation: Whenever we are blessed in life, especially regarding finances, we should not boast. Nor should we tell everyone because a jealous or hateful person can become a real danger to you.

2

"dawg no howl if im ha bone"

Translation: The dog does not howl if he has a bone.

Explanation: The dog is an animal that loves bones and gets very comfortable when it has bones to chew on. Similarly, people do not become troubled or distressed when they are comfortable.

3

"if yu noh mash ants, yu noh fine him guts"

Translation: If you do not smash an ant, it is impossible for you to find its guts.

Explanation: If you do not have a close bond with a person (through times both good and bad *and especially bad*), then you aren't able to know them thoroughly.

4

"ole fiyah tick easy fe ketch"

Translation: Old firesticks are easily rekindled.

Explanation: It is easier to light logs that have been burnt before than to start a fire with fresh logs. Likewise, if a relationship has previously existed between two people, it is easier to rekindle the flames of love than to start a new relationship with someone else.

5

"chicken merry, hawk deh near"

Translation: The chicken, unaware of the danger posed by the hovering hawk, makes merry.

Explanation: Look, I'm as human as the next person. Sometimes *"Ignorance is Bliss"*. But in our happiness and comfort, we should also remember to be aware of our surroundings and the people closest to us.

6

"yu caan sidung pan cow bak an cuss cow kin"

Translation: You cannot sit on the back of the cow and curse the skin of the cow.

Explanation: At some point in life, most, if not all of us will need a helping hand. When we get back on our feet, we should not speak negatively or in a derogatory way about that person. Nor should we turn our back on such a person.

7

"yu shake man han, but yu noh shake im hawt"

Translation: You can shake a man's head, but you cannot shake his heart.

Explanation: You'll never know what someone truly thinks of you by simply being in their presence. Therefore, pay close attention to their words and actions.

8

"fiyah deh a muss-muss tail, im tink a cool breeze"

Translation: There is a fire blowing at the tail of the mouse, but he believes he is feeling the effects of a cooling breeze.

Explanation: *"Ignorance is Bliss"* strikes again. And sometimes we're so blissfully ignorant we don't see or search for any hints of danger until we are overwhelmed.

9

"when chubble tek yu, pickney shut fit yu"

Translation: When you find yourself in trouble, a child's shirt fits you.

Explanation: There's no way a child and a grown man would fit into the same size shirt unless, of course, that child is an NBA prospect. However, when we find ourselves in trouble, we greatly appreciate any help that can be given, no matter how small. If you've ever been in trouble, you know what I mean.

10

"wha gwan bad a maanin, caan kum gud a evenin"

Translation: What went wrong in the morning cannot be remedied in the evening.

Explanation: At some point, we'll all face some sizeable situations in life, be they physical, financial, or otherwise. The smart thing to do is create the best solutions we can for those situations. Also, the ongoing issue more than likely took some time to get to that point, so we must be patient and trust the process.

11
"big blanket mek man sleep late"

Translation: A thick blanket causes a man to sleep late.

Explanation: An over-abundance of luxuries causes one to become complacent and to take life's blessings for granted.

12
"wha sweet a mout' hat a belly"

Translation: What tastes sweet in the mouth burns the belly.

Explanation: Some things (and people) are not good for us, although they appear to be exactly what we want. We should be cautious about who and what we attach ourselves to. Otherwise, it will lead to a lot of pain and embarrassment.

13

"me come yah fe drink milk, me noh come yah fe count cow"

Translation: I came here to drink milk, not to count cows.

Explanation: Apply this saying to many instances in your personal life, especially at work. Do the job you're paid to do and leave all other affairs that don't concern you alone.

14

"pit inna de sky, it fall inna yuh y'eye"

Translation: If you spit in the sky, it falls into your eye.

Explanation: Whatever energy you put out in the world eventually makes its way back to you. Make sure you treat others well.

15
"yu cyaan ketch quaku, ketch im shut"

Translation: If you cannot catch Quaku (Harry), catch his shirt.

Explanation: It is not always possible to get everything you want. Be satisfied with whatever you have until you are able to get all you want.

16
"payshent man ride danki"

Translation: A patient man rides a donkey.

Explanation: It is customary that travelers in a great hurry hate to go with the slow but sure donkey. For them, a horse used to galloping at terrific speeds for sustained periods seems to be a more logical choice. However, although much slower, the donkey eventually gets to its journey's end. Similarly, we must exercise great patience to reach our goals.

17
"waant aal, lose aal"

Translation: If you want everything you see, you will eventually lose all.

Explanation: Take just what you can comfortably manage rather than trying to grab everything. If you can't control yourself, greed will eventually destroy you.

18

"chubble deh a bush, anancy cyah i'kum a yaad"

Translation: There is trouble in the business, and Anancy takes it home.

Explanation: Anancy, the folk hero of West African origin, is never satisfied with leaving things in their proper place. He sometimes takes home the spoils of his foraging, many times to the unhappiness of his family. What does not concern us is that we should leave strictly alone.

19
"wanti wanti cyaan getti, an getti getti noh wanti"

Translation: He who wants it desperately cannot get it; he who get it easily does not want it or appreciate it.

Explanation: Be thankful for the blessings that come to you, always realizing that many of the things we take for granted are luxuries to others.

20

"new broom sweep clean, but owl broom noe dem cahna"

Translation: The new broom sweeps clean, but the old broom knows all the corners.

Explanation: We should strive for a happy blend between the old and the new, combining the new's freshness with the senior's valuable experience.

21

"mischiff kum by de poun' an' go by de ownse"

Translation: Mischief comes by the pound and goes by the ounce.

Explanation: Mischief makers can stir up a tremendous amount of trouble with only a few words or maybe one action. The effects of this can be challenging to minimize and even more difficult to fix. Let us not be mischief-makers. We could hurt ourselves and others irreparably.

22

"poun' ah fret cyaan pay ownse ah dett"

Translation: One pound of fretting cannot repay one ounce of debt.

Explanation: Problems are not solved by worrying. The time spent fretting could be more gainfully spent on considering workable alternatives and solutions.

23

"willful wase bring woeful want"

Translation: Willful waste brings woeful want.

Explanation: Don't willfully waste what you have, or you could end up bitterly regretting what you wasted when you find yourself in need.

24

"noh buy puss inna bag"

Translation: Do not purchase a pussycat in a bag.

Explanation: Examine carefully whatever you purchase or accept from someone else. In matters of the head and heart, do not be quick to accept a person as the "genuine article", without a thorough investigation.

25
"mek wan jackass bray"

Translation: Allow one jackass (donkey) to bray at a time.

Explanation: It is difficult to see the merit in other people's ideas if everybody attempts to speak simultaneously. Also, if someone is speaking foolishly, avoid adding to the confusion.

26

"quatti buy chubble, hunjed poun cyaan pay farri"

Translation: A penny-halfpenny (11/2d) buys trouble; one hundred pounds (£100) cannot pay for it.

Explanation: Little blunders can cause us to find ourselves in complex situations that we cannot extricate ourselves from.

27
"lang run, shaat ketch"

Translation: Long run, short catch.

Explanation: It may take a long while for you to be caught and punished for wrongdoing, but you will be caught one day. *Karmas is always on the move, one way or another.*

28
"wan han wash de oda"

Translation: One hand washes the other.

Explanation: One nice gesture deserves another.

29

"de more yu luk, de less yu si"

Translation: The more you look, the less you will see.

Explanation: It is impossible to know every single detail about any matter. Also, the more you find out, the less you know.

30
"no matta how kokruch junk, im noh waak pass fowl yaad"

Translation: No matter how drunk the cockroach becomes, he never makes the mistake of walking past the yard of the fowl.

Explanation: The cockroach is considered a delicacy for fowls. In the interest of self-preservation, cockroaches are reluctant to go past any area where a fowl may easily catch him. For humans, the same principle should apply, self-preservation being the first law of the of the species.

31
"hag nyam wha im myne gi im fah"

Translation: The hog/pig eats whatever its mind gives it for (or wants).

Explanation: To each his own.

32

"bowl go, packy come"

Translation: Bowl goes, calabash comes.

Explanation: It was a widespread occurrence in traditional Jamaican life to see covered dishes carrying some delicious meal being borne by a child and bound for some neighbor's home. It was also customary, although certainly not mandatory, for the bearer to return with something for the sender, perhaps in a picky (calabash scraped and used as a bowl). Also, one nice gesture deserves another.

33
"wan finga cyaan kill louse"

Translation: One finger alone cannot kill lice.

Explanation: Co-operation is necessary for projects involving more than one person.

34

"yuh pred yuh bed haad, yu haffi liddung pan i'haad"

Translation: If you spread your bed hard, you must lie on a hard bed.

Explanation: You must accept responsibility for your actions; whatever you sow, you will surely reap.

35

"no mug no bruk, no cawfee no dash weh"

Translation: The mug is not broken; therefore, the coffee is not thrown away (or wasted).

Explanation: Even in the most difficult of times, if total devastation has not occurred, one should count his or her blessings. Do not blow simple matters out of proportion.

36
"ebry puss hab im 4 o'clock"

Translation: Every cat has his 4 o'clock.

Explanation: We should not behave as if we are better than others or allow our position in life to blind us to the fact that tremendous opportunities can be given to those persons whom we would least expect to reap these benefits. ("Your day will come.")

37

"wen mawga plantin wan fi dead, im shoot"

Translation: When a meager plantain wants to die, it shoots.

Explanation: After a plantain tree shoots and bears a bunch of familiar fruit, it ends its helpful life and dies after that. Applied to humans - when we are no longer concerned about the safety of our persons, the preservation of our good character of job or family, then we are too apt to behave stupidly.

38
"wen coco ripe, im mus buss"

Translation: When the cocoa (cacao) ripens, it bursts.

Explanation: It is easy to identify the intentions of an individual by his or her actions.

39
"wen man belly full, im bruck pat"

Translation: When a man's belly is filled, he breaks the pot.

Explanation: When man is satisfied, he often forgets what hunger or need is and will be indifferent to the sources of his assistance until he again finds himself in need.

40
"wa de goat du, de kid falla"

Translation: What the goat does, the kid follows.

Explanation: Children absorb behavioral cues from their parents and other significant adults in their lives. We should set good examples for our children.

41
"yu neva see smoke widout fiyah"

Translation: You never see smoke without fire.

Explanation: Sometimes, actions that appear to be trivial are actually indications of some deep-rooted resentment or of trouble or romance brewing.

42

"tek whey yuh get tell yu get whey yu want"

Translation: Take what you can get until you can get what you want.

Explanation: Every opportunity, well used, can be a stepping stone to the realization of your ultimate goals.

43

"ef yu cyaan get turkey, yu haffi satisfy wid jancro"

Translation: If you are unable to get turkey, then you must be satisfied with John Crow.

Explanation: No well-thinking Jamaican would be "caught dead" with a portion of crow's meat on his plate. However, this proverb simply advises us to be prepared to accept situations that we may not like for the sake of peace. Sometimes, second best is not so bad after all.

44
"parson christen him own pickney first"

Translation: The Parson always christens his own child first.

Explanation: Charity begins at home.

45
"when ashes cold dog sleep dere"

Translation: When the ashes are cold, even a dog can sleep there.

Explanation: Circumstances alter cases.

46

"alligator lay egg, but him no fowl"

Translation: The alligator lays eggs, but he is not a fowl.

Explanation: Never look at a subject from just one point of view.

47

"cry-cry picney neva hab him right"

Translation: A crybaby (for a stubborn) never gets his rights.

Explanation: Those who are always complaining are seldom listened to.

48

"nanny goat neva scratch him back till him see wall"

Translation: A he-goat never wants to scratch his back till he sees a stone wall.

Explanation: Await the proper opportunity.

49

"rockstone a rivva bottom no feel sun hot"

Translation: A stone at the bottom of the river never feels the heat of the sun.

Explanation: Those in easy circumstances do not realize the hardship of others.

50

"ebry day da fishing day, but ebry day no fe catch fish"

Translation: Every day's fishing day, but not every day's a day to catch fish.

Explanation: Reward does not always follow labor.

51

"hungry hungry and full full no trabel same pass"

Translation: The Hungry belly and the full belly do not walk the same road.

Explanation: The poor man and the rich man go in different directions.

52

"shoes alone know if stocking hab hole"

Translation: Shoes alone know if the stocking has holes.

Explanation: The wearer alone knows where the shoe pinches.

53

"good frien betta dan packet money"

Translation: A good friend is better than money in the pocket.

Explanation: No matter how valuable our material possessions may be to us, a good friend, especially in times of trouble, is often proven to be worth more. We should treasure our friends not only recognizing them when we are in need.

54

"bifoe gud food pwile, meck belly bus"

Translation: Before allowing good food to spoil, allow the belly to burst.

Explanation: Taken literally, this proverb could see the demise of many persons who are unable to control their appetite. However, the moral behind this old saying is that one should make every good use of life's opportunities; also, never waste or discard today that you or someone else may be able to use tomorrow.

55

"tu much ratta neva dig gud hole"

Translation: Too many rats never dug a good hole.

Explanation: A good job/project/activity could be spoilt if there are too many individuals attempting to carry out the same task. Ideally, work should be delegated, and one should avoid frustrating those who can really do the job by gently re-deploying those who are timewasters.

56
"self-praise a no rekumendayshan"

Translation: Self-praise is no recommendation

Explanation: The Bible advises, "Let another man praise thee, and not thine own lips" (Proverbs 27:2). If we announce only recommendations of our own worth, then it is inevitable that such announcements are mere vanity. One should be too quick to "sound his own trumpet".

57

"a no evryting kum fram abuv a blessen"

Translation: Not everything that comes from above is a blessing.

Explanation: Enjoy those blessings that come from above, but remember that many people you see did not get those same "blessings" by being righteous. *Remember, the devil gives out blessings too.*

58

"wen po' git up, im tun chubble tu de wole"

Translation: When the poor man gets up, he becomes trouble to the world.

Explanation: The elevation of someone who used to be disdained or sneered at by others could be cause for much disturbance in the minds of those who did not wish him well.

59
"rain neva fall a one man door"

Translation: Rain never falls at one man's door.

Explanation: When it rains, it rains on all. "Rain" here could also be seen as "blessings", be it money, property, etc., as is seen in the scriptures where both good and bad people are blessed (Matthew 5:45) "Sendeth rain on the just and the unjust."

60
"john crow neva make house till rain come"

Translation: John Crow never thinks of making his house until it rains.

Explanation: Some people never make provision for a "rainy day".

61

"stranger no know where da deep water in de pass"

Translation: A stranger does not know where the deep water is.

Explanation: A caution against undertaking to do something you don't fully understand.

62
"sleep hab no massa"

Translation: Sleep has no master.

Explanation: Sooner or later, you must sleep.

63

"john crow tink him own pickney white"

Translation: Young John crows are white when hatched but do not remain white.

Explanation: What is one's own is always the best.

64
"too much si-dun bruk breeches"

Translation: Sitting down too many wears out one's trousers.

Explanation: Idleness leads to wants.

65

"woman mout an fowl a one"

Translation: A woman has a mouth like a fowl.

Explanation: Women love to talk, and talk, and talk, lol.

66
"no mek one donkey choke you"

Translation: Don't let one donkey choke you.

Explanation: Do not be misled by a fool.

67

"darg among doctor, cockroach among shaver"

Translation: A dog among doctors, a cockroach among shavers.

Explanation: Stick to the surroundings to which you are most fitted.

68

"if you can get turkey you must sati'fy wid john crow"

Translation: If you can't get turkey, you must be satisfied with John Crow.

Explanation: If you cannot get what you want, you must be satisfied with that which comes nearest to it in appearance.

69
"driva flag him wife fus"

Translation: The driver flogs his own wife first.

Explanation: If you're going to execute true justice, don't show favoritism to anyone.

70

"finga neva say "look here," him say "look yonder"

Translation: Finger never says, "Look here," he says, "Look yonder."

Explanation: People do not usually point out their own faults.

71

"if you get your han in a devil mout tek it out"

Translation: If you place your hand in the devil's mouth, take it out carefully.

Explanation: Act with caution/wisdom in getting out of a complex or dangerous situation.

72

"peacock hide him foot when him hear bout him tail"

Translation: The peacock hides his foot when he hears about his tail.

Explanation: A proud person doesn't like their flaws, however small, being seen.

73

"no wait till drum beat before you grine you axe"

Translation: Do not wait until the drumbeats before you grind your axe.

Explanation: Don't wait for the perfect time to appear to accomplish your dreams. Instead, look at what you've got right now and build with that.

74

"you fraid fe yeye, you neva nyam head"

Translation: If you are afraid of the eye, you will never eat the head.

Explanation: If you pay the opinion of everyone with too much respect, you will never be successful.

75

"a no want a fat mek nightingale foot 'tan' so"

Translation: It is not for the want of fat that the nightingale's legs stand the way they do.

Explanation: Do not judge by appearances; things may not be as they seem.

76

"evry day devil help teef; wan day gad wi help watchman"

Translation: Every day, the devil helps the thief; one day, God will help the watchman.

Explanation: There are probably very few things in this world more infuriating than seeing evil people who, through various forms of treachery, become rich, powerful or both. However, God was and is always aware of everything. He will ensure that the work done by the good is rewarded.

77

"cowad man kip soun bone"

Translation: A cowardly man keeps sound bones.

Explanation: Remember, as tough as you are or think you are, there's someone more challenging. That tougher person may also have absolutely nothing to lose while you do, so sometimes, walking away is the best decision you can make.